Several years ago, a friend of mine who is one of the too-rare woman leading engineering teams at some of the biggest tech companies told me that when interviewing for new software engineers, she asked about their creative pursuits. In her experience, the best engineers were also musicians, writers, crafters, artists.

Evoking and referencing sci-fi and science, fables and fantasy, technology and trauma, code and culture, Betsy Aoki's *Breakpoint* is a unique techno-literary work, and I hope it introduces techno-lit as a genre. *Breakpoint* unveils what those of us in the world of tech, like my friend, have long known, contrary to popular belief: Creating innovative tech is equal parts art and science.

You don't have to work in tech to experience technology as inextricably intertwined with your life. Aoki captures it as an ever-presence, for good and bad, in our work, relationships, health, and even our memory. *Breakpoint* is haunting, as I find all good sci-fi to be, and it is visceral, as excellent drama is. Like the very best code, *Breakpoint* is also both clean and beautiful, with no word or command wasted.

Elisa Camahort Page, Entrepreneur and Author, *Road Map for Revolutionaries: Resistance, Activism, and Advocacy for All*

In *Breakpoint*, Betsy Aoki sharpens the nerves of her poems, applying, brilliantly, the terse grammar of computer code to family immigration stories, from detention camp incarceration to the speaker's "coder-girl" design for a game in which female characters use combat as an unapologetic mode of self-making—all cast against the glaringly white backdrop of Silicon Valley. Aoki's poems are restless, allusive, spikey, mournful, mystical, yearning, lovely, and always *always* open to the attention and sway of language over time.

—Dorothy Barresi, Judge of Patricia Bibby First Book Award
and Author of *What We Did While We Made More Guns*

BREAKPOINT

Winner of Patricia Bibby First Book Award

BREAKPOINT

BETSY AOKI

TEBOT BACH • HUNTINGTON BEACH • CALIFORNIA • 2022

Front cover illustration by: Yejin Park "THIS WAY UP"
Author photo by: Jessica L. Drake, JLD Imagery
Book design by: Russel Davis, Gray Dog Press, Spokane, WA

ISBN-10: 1-939678-95-1
ISBN-13: 978-1-939678-95-9

A Tebot Bach book
Tebot Bach, Welsh for little teapot, is a Nonprofit Public Benefit
Corporation, which sponsors workshops, forums, lectures, and
publications. Tebot Bach books are distributed by Small Press
Distribution.

The Tebot Bach Mission: Advancing literacy, strengthening
community, and transforming life experiences with the power of
poetry through readings, workshops, and publications.

This book is made possible by a generous donation from
Steven R. and Lera B. Smith.

www.tebotbach.org

For all the women in tech making it happen

Contents

SECTION ONE

SECTION TWO

SECTION THREE

SECTION ONE

In reality we'd almost never want to use destroy with anything but pointers, in the first place…given that it turns things back into raw memory and all.

228 #This collision, defined

```
229   def collide (self,other_object):
230
231   x = self.get_radius ( )
232   y = other_object.get_radius ( )
233   raddistance = x + y
234
235   if dist (self.pos,other_object.pos) < raddistance:
236       return True
237   else:
238       return False
```

The tires hold the road on their rims

My scars have no brakes.
My scars carve me round.
I want you, like I wanted black rims
and silver spokes, yellow mustard on the tongue
and the blue vinyl seat of things I can't name.
I want you like I once dreaded dark shadows
the depths of bushes where we thought
the swamp monster stayed all night.
I suppose I want the monster too.
        **

I want you, like a banyan grows
around a host tree, a green memory,
and then as the host dies inside
winds tree fingers in a spiral of leathery leaves,
holding the center space hollow.

I am ready to touch the lines of your face.
I am ready as a bicycle
to be stolen.

Walking here is to be swallowed by the sky
—For the Topaz Museum opening July 2017

1.
bits of wood and wall board outline a family in the dirt

                        it is important not to become bitter grandpa said
                            as his eyes looked away to a time where the ground

turned to terrible soup when it rained snow falling through slats

          then he died   his sons went back to see what became of youth spent
                  with barbed wire and dog's teeth   a man shot for walking

too close to the wires. now the wind has nothing to be outside of

                                    this desert has nothing to stop it
                                 it can't happen here again, you say

no more huddled bodies, no more small boys throwing rocks at the fence

2.
If you can only think of twin towers falling, remember Topaz
    internment camp
opened on Sept. 11, 1942, its mouth wide as the desert sky.
    Open
hate shoving suitcases spilled onto the sidewalk.   Slurs
tracked into the fields like fertilizer.   Splash
of green on slate rocks and white dust.   Epithets
scattered everywhere like the bits of trash   no one bothered
with coat hangers, broken cold cream jars, kids' marbles
    when they left
piles of nails crunch underfoot   weeds tumble
    between buildings

no longer there, a testament to what people   believed
    could change

millions of years ago   this desert was a sea, and at night
    with nothing
to do but fear   my grandmother made seashells into
    necklaces
they keep trying to tell you   looping
I once was wet, grew fish with iridescent scales   now stark
memories are powdered bone in a cage   on a string,
    whorls
break the hinges   let all these silent   birds
fly home to roost

One hundred ways to say you in Japanese

You.
Everything is ricochet
and pinion flare, soft silk billowing
around a shape in the wind,
the you. Understood. あなた means I see you
liquid, formal. *Wakarimasen ka?*
(This you never spoken.)
Understand that the you over there
is far from casual. Lower status to upper.

The you
over here by me, breathless;
sometimes depending
on the region. That word can mean
I and not you. Also the *you*
you call your mother; she *is you* for a second
in the window rain, slicking over the moments
with a coating of slate tiles and scarlet.

The *you*
of all the letters – so fresh-faced, so gorgeous in gloves
and you as my teacher, so stern
and full of folders. Slim just
fits one word into the files, oh the you
of plenty of paper, plenty of oh
narrow winding roads.

Oh my comic book enemy,
my solo self, sometimes I. *It's you.*
We are only. Mirrored/Words.
That phrase is so you, so many
kinds of you. That anime cartoon

shakes her fist, rides her
skateboard silver-streaked.
That young gangster slouches
into the wind, inside the cigarette
you burning
at its end.

Okuri Inu, or the sending-off dog demon

Japanese legends say you will meet your dark dog like a friend,
like a man too concerned for your welfare, like a host
with a wooden lantern who can only light part of your way together,
sending you off only so far as it is safe. But unlike a host who returns home,
certain he knows good girls and bad, certain how soft the road is,
certain nothing dire could ever come to you because
you don't deserve it, the dark dog follows.
The dark dog does not talk of deserving, he grins and growls for all,
metacarpals matching you tread for tread, pad-fall for footfall,
bushy tail wagging behind like a wolf's. Perhaps he is a cute puppy
who follows as if in love, as if trailing to make sure you get home.
Chi, chi, chi trills the yosuzume, bird-certain that a slavering
heavy beast follows you through the dark, urging you not to stumble.
Twisted roots conspire to catch toes and heels on each step on the path,
the canopy of what people don't want to see at night
blocking the stars, the moon. Few could believe someone
so kindly as he's been, has teeth. Then you slip,
and the world is as black as the inside of a closed mouth,
hot and sticky with blood from a bitten tongue.
The night is as frantic as the breath through your nostrils.
As rapid-fire as the word no. Nonononono.
The lore advises to fake the fall if you stumble, pretend intent,
rest your panic out until you can keep going. But little sister
I can only tell you what I know: I did not keep my steps perfect.
I met his eyes with my knife, and complicit silence
with anger. I became more than his mouthful.

Because you know and I know what real friends do,
and by the dog's body still lying on the road,
what he did was not it.

Encapsulation in computer programming

Plants close off portions of themselves to bear their seeds;
think on the milkweed pod bursting its fuzzy halos
over a field to the fringes of encapsulation.

I've sealed myself into medicines that I have taken –
poisons carefully applied, sealed in their gelatin shells,
and worn down by the life of the intestine to burst
a dose, a remedy, a balm. A bomb

can encapsulate the fate of a woman.
Someday Space X might present me as its aviatrix
to Mars. And I'll toss on the heap of memory
everything I couldn't keep, that I couldn't hide

inside shadows of class structure, nor perfect
with noose and cowl and spacesuit,
any of my illusions of running slowly through time.

The decimal is a heartbeat; it can stop itself, or repeat

The first thing to know about this language
is how it laces up memory, cinches memory up in a bale,
hay golden across an umber field.
You know how much you can carry in your hands?
　　The first one's a string, a cat's cradle crisscrossing all the lines on your palms.
You know how much you can carry in your purse?
　　The second one's an integer, crammed with usefulness and shine, too much
　　nail polish on these numbers; when you cry they won't break.
You know how much memory you packed in the back
of a Honda Civic, fleeing the next broken bone,
jealous rage, crashing bottle? Remember how infinity went,
lines of the highway hugging the land like a sister?
　　That last one's the float, up to and including the rounding
of the sun that set over the shitty motel you hid at,
then sped to some town that smelled of batter and burning tires,
　　　　　　integers like miles pouring into the horizon.

```
120    #many to many collisions


121
122    def group_group_collide (group1,group2):
123        global score, explosion_group
124        collision_counter = 0
125        copygroup1= group1
126        for j in copygroup1:
127            if group_collide(group2,j)== True:
128                collision_counter+=1
129                score = score+1
130                group1.discard(j)
```

There is no new world without a girl leaping and fighting

Bare feet press into the earth, harder, then harder again.
Nothing cuts through callous like time. Nothing cuts
through skin like remembrance. Nothing shields
like an elbow block to his gut
and a kick to the knees. Go low. Go high.

Everything around here flies and will hurt you.
Camera tightens to the body jerk, the skull crack, the fall
and skid across blood-stained floors. If I told you
my life was all wires unseen, a crane above my head
winding upward with some swift hope – would you be surprised?

A Japanese girl can catch her breath when the spiral to full
time in the air completes, then does a side kick
to the jaw in two shots: first, the heel of her shoe
to his face and then another camera flash in his eyes
as he staggers back into the grumbling bitter

granularity of horror. Harrowing beads of sweat
carve out the lines of her face. The woman she becomes
will fight this aerial, invisible opponent in your eyes,
all your headwinds of bruised and bleeding disbelief.
No. There is no new world without a girl leaping.

Standing in the Xbox building parking lot

Blurred within ninja video, slicing an arm to bone seems so easy.
A guy walks by her with a cigarette cloud for a head.
Virtual splashes of blue X's and yellow skulls
leading to his oily motorcycle, red leather flames
licking his black pants. She is standing
in the building's parking lot wondering
if she has breast cancer and if so,
how to tell him, the boss.
So surreal to be on the cell miles away
from the 20 TVs stacked in her cubicle, talking
to a nurse about the lump that ticks like a grenade
in Gears of War under her armpit.

Don't blink, whispers the world.

She taps, puts on extra lipstick, listening
in girl camo and corporate face as the nurse drones,
Don't wear deodorant before the extra mammogram.
Has she made space for invader after invader
under the casual chill of decades?
There must be a better word for godspeed and godmode
and the crash that changes your life for good.

After hearing the terror she will go back to the war
targeting deep inside the steel and glass
where walls of people code and collide,
where there is no such thing as a perfect shadow
perfect water, or perfect tears. Just perfect breasts.

Do I look like I code?

This is what [X_]'s code looks like:
a teletype explodes after eating a dictionary.

This is what coding looks like from behind:
knob over knob of spine hunched over

tympani beat, flat Chiclet clicks,
uneasy buttocks shifting on a hard seat.

This is what [X_] coding looks like:
a shiny silver glow, a dull matte black square,

knob over knob hunched over tufts of hair,
fingers of light across a naked throat.

This is what happens when you code for [X_]:

<   >
Whatever you held in that space I erase.

Tender Buttons of the Computer Age

Not clicky, not piston, not python, not pebbles we picked up on the beach. Not the talk on my phone, not the mute, not print screen. Made of wool, cotton, leather, silk. Made of skin, nerve, muscle stretched thin. Flushed with blood. All you can look at when my face is up here.

What language, what version

A computer is full of parrot, and pieces of eight. What pirates sail these seas, unblinking, scurvy-kneed and sure of the tongue their mother spoke. There is always an earlier version that was better, with better coordinates of reference. There is always to the future to look forward to.

A method of a class

A hammer thrown at spiders and no exceptions, a call where the answer
is always come, a riddle of a verb babbling by idiots of silicon, 0, 1, 0.
Underneath the hood of all our skins will be this hexadecimal patterning,
this silver idiot wire, this murmur of simplicity like a lady's skirt that once
lifted always rises to complexity.

Debugging

An open window where all the sense flown out and feathers mark the fail.

103 #helper to process collisions

```
104   def group_collide(group,other_object):
105   collision_counter= 0
106   copyset= set(group)
107   for i in copyset:
108      #using copy of main set
109      if i.collide(other_object):
110              #asteroid explodes as ship hits it
111              collision_counter+=1
112              new_explosion = Sprite(i.pos, i.vel, 0,      i.angle_vel,
                          explosion_image, explosion_info)
113              explosion_group.add (new_explosion)
114              explosion_sound.play()
115                  #removing from real deal
116                  group.remove(i)
117                  return True
```

Buruburu

When the blood and the hate in the eyes
of your foes became too much, when the shine
of blades became dulled in the dust,
when the opening between snarled bodies
desperate for survival offered, you fled –

and the buruburu
ate. It dined upon the shakes
in your legs as you forded
the wide river. It nibbled at
the ever-increasing beat
of your heart that knew
when it is lucky not to fight.

It placed both hands on your shoulders and neck
and froze your face solid, swung you from a tree
with a rope made of your hair.

Dizzy, swinging, corpse
made an example, coward
bleating in the wind,
you yourself became a buruburu,
speeding back along ruts in the road

to the same battlefield you left. Hands icy
white, uniform now tattered
to bleached bones
and empty gaps between rags.

Now you are the frigid wind
upon the nape of the neck
of the last man

crouched inside a hollow,
hating war with his last breath
but unable to fight it.

Brother, you whisper into his shiver.
Brother.

Breakpoint
by Betsy Aoki

Winner of Tebot Bach's
Patricia Bibby First Book Award

69 pages ~ $17.00 paper original

ISBN: 978-1-939678-95-9
PUB DATE: March, 1, 2022 from Small Press Distribution (spd.org)
MEDIA CONTACT: Alexandra Umlas. Alexandraumlas@gmail.com

Dedicated to, "all the women in tech making it happen," *Breakpoint* by Betsy Aoki is a debut poetry collection that combines intense lyrical free verse with found Python "code poems" to explore the modern technological and societal landscape. Aoki's poems bring the reader into her world of polygons and fractals, Japanese folklore and family stories, computational language and robot factories, and the timeless yearning to be truly seen. Machines speak in this book, as do the women in tech's voices, voices that bring home what it's like to be the only one of your kind in the rooms where the future is being made.

Of the book's signature poem, "Slouching like a velvet rope":
"This poem unwinds towards unexpected shifts and turns in just a few lines. And it manages a kind of lyric punch at the mention of each image."
-Jericho Brown, winner of the Pulitzer Prize for *The Tradition* and judge for the 2021 Auburn Witness Poetry Prize

Aoki captures [technology] as an ever-presence, for good and bad, in our work, relationships, health, and even our memory. *Breakpoint* is haunting, as I find all good sci-fi to be, and it is visceral, as excellent drama is. Like the very best code, *Breakpoint* is also both clean and beautiful, with no word or command wasted.
 -Elisa Camahort Page, co-founder of *BlogHer*

"Aoki has magically brought the technological — and in her hands, playful — language of computing into the realm of poetry: breakpoint, collide, return— and of course, code. Her poems using digital diction are quirky and adamant – here is a woman in a male-dominated field staking her territory in real life and in metaphor.
 -Kimiko Hahn, Author of *Foreign Bodies*

"Aoki sharpens the nerves of her poems, applying, brilliantly, the terse grammar of computer code to family immigration stories, from detention camp incarceration to the speaker's "coder-girl" design for a game in which female characters use combat as an unapologetic mode of self-making—all cast against the glaringly white backdrop of Silicon Valley. Aoki's poems are restless, allusive, spiky, mournful, mystical, yearning, lovely, and always always open to the attention and sway of language over time."
 -Dorothy Barresi, Judge of Patricia Bibby First Book Award and author of *What We Did While We Made More Guns*

"Much like a word problem, [these] poems underscore the way we store and retrieve details. Of the many ways we can remember – sound, taste, smell, texture – coding allows us to leave a trail in the chaos of random experiences where those details may be easily reached and reassembled. Reminiscent of Alice Fulton's *Fractal Poetics*, these poems assemble, conflate and arrange: what we know, what we feel, and what we remember. You don't have to be a coder to know it's love when memory and language share the same equation."
 -Colleen J. McElroy's latest collection of poems, *BLOOD MEMORY*, was listed as a Paterson Poetry Award selection.

Betsy Aoki is author of *Breakpoint* (Tebot Bach, 2022). She lives in Seattle, Washington. https://betsyaoki.com/

To order visit: bit.ly/breakpoint2022

TEBOT BACH   Tebot Bach: PO Box 7887, Huntington Beach, California, 92615

Buruburu

When the blood and the hate in the eyes
of your foes became too much, when the shine
of blades became dulled in the dust,
when the opening between snarled bodies
desperate for survival offered, you fled –

and the buruburu
ate. It dined upon the shakes
in your legs as you forded
the wide river. It nibbled at
the ever-increasing beat
of your heart that knew
when it is lucky not to fight.

It placed both hands on your shoulders and neck
and froze your face solid, swung you from a tree
with a rope made of your hair.

Dizzy, swinging, corpse
made an example, coward
bleating in the wind,
you yourself became a buruburu,
speeding back along ruts in the road

to the same battlefield you left. Hands icy
white, uniform now tattered
to bleached bones
and empty gaps between rags.

Now you are the frigid wind
upon the nape of the neck
of the last man

crouched inside a hollow,
hating war with his last breath
but unable to fight it.

Brother, you whisper into his shiver.
Brother.

Playing Halo 3 in Iraq

He is Black, covered in tan camouflage
with fingerless gloves like a prize-fighter's, smiling
between me and a woman on an airplane bound for Seattle.
 After 27 hours in the air, he speaks with precision:

"ma'am" – "please" – "excuse me."

When I tell this Army man
I work on an indie games team,
tired pride gleams from the steel rims of his spectacles.

He slipped around Internet restrictions to figure out
how to hold tournaments that include Master Chief.
From one end of a gymnasium to another, end to end
his buddies played: No smacktalk between teams,

just smackdown and gunfire.

We talk about the foods he has had on his list for two weeks
of civilian life – fresh veggies, fresh fruit but mostly
one big juicy steak. Not too much eating though, as he's going back.

He's lost 60 lbs. in the desert, on purpose, through diet
and this mixed martial arts training where you must always fight
one against many for the right to stand up.

You do not go far with silence

You are the car that haunts my dreams: my foot
      atop the gas pedal, pulse pulse pushing us forward

      toward a yellow glow, a green sign, a place to stop
and rest and then the wrench light glows by the steering wheel.

You shudder as I drive you, a fusion of gears and prayers,
      oil and ordinary fear, the road slick-slickens with the fluid

we are leaking together, murderous car, treacherous
      throttle body giving out, sudden acceleration at a stop light.

I know you are trying to kill me, and all I can do
      is recall your deep sleek form forming in the driveway

dormant, recall your leather interior smelling sweetly
      of newness and spice, recall your draining out

every cent in my bank account and still you want more –

What to expect from the Hadron Collider as a college roommate

It will probably not be home for supper anytime soon.
Things will get broken and not put back together again.
When you speak to it about paying its fair share of the rent,

it will start at you with that far-away look, or as though it is

squinting at things too small for you to see. Let it,
but go through its pockets on rent day. It will probably
have a million dollars you didn't notice before.

Do not answer when it asks you for a Higgs Boson,

or where your girlfriend went, as it is hooked
on speed. If it doesn't get all of its jeans out of the dryer,
it won't notice if you mail them to the lab posthaste.

The Hadron Collider is always working late.

No, professors will not hold you accountable.
It will always be wearing the t-shirt that says:
See or be seen. You will punch it in the arm

for joy when it finally remembers your name.

A tenjō kudari ("ceiling hanger" yōkai) defends her theft

at night I hover above the beams you've hammered
between heaven and your spread silk coverlet

the air, which is nothing to you, is everything to me
the wood, which is something hard to you, is nothing to me

I slip fingers beyond the pine knots and holding on to breezes
with my other hand see the dust dancing between the straw

reach down for your sleeping face

eager for your exhalations   those moist, warm castoffs
they are spirals of rips   bits of soft driftwood

eddying out from your body   discarded as casually
as you threw down my bones wrapped in kimono-rags

cast away as you did your horse fleeing on the road
from my father's huntsmen   its lungs bursting   beneath your body

nightly your dead horse and I call to each other strung singing
as we are from bough and beam sometimes hanging   still as skulls

above your head   as you sleep, as you ride, as you love
others far better than you ever loved us

tonight is the farthest I have ever stretched from the rafters
listening from the hackberry tree the horse whinnies in the cold

your eyelids flicker open as my cold lips fall on yours
no she does not even roll over as I steal your last breath

SECTION TWO

For whichever resource we are interested in bounding — time, memory, so on —we define the intrinsic complexity of a problem as the complexity of the most efficient algorithm that solves it.

87 # helper functions to handle transformations

```
88
89   def angle_to_vector(ang):
90       return [math.cos(ang), math.sin(ang)]
91
92   def dist(p, q):
93       return math.sqrt((p[0]- q[0]) ** 2 + (p[1]- q[1]) ** 2)
```

Stack

We are watching your body vault
pivot and erase words

of smoke. You push yourself in
and I pop out. Bury*, says Turing
and Unbury. Seen, and unseeing.

I think they forgot
there was a woman in there.

*Tech note: Whereas today we use other terms to denote getting data in and
out of the call stack (push, pull, pop), or when talking about the data type,
Alan Turing used Bury and Unbury as the means of calling to/from computer
program subroutines.*

For a heartbeat

He begins by shoveling forgetfulness,
October images of tired retinas, irises,
floating lights. The taste of cold tobacco drives him
spitting from Eden. The taste of this day drives cloud blades

across the evening. The tease of her body drives him
through the walls of his head clambering down vines
with hairy leaves, silver ivy curling
above his forelock. He has escaped for now

inside his head to a place she cannot reach
for a heartbeat. He runs and runs
by the field of *I'll Meet You There*
passing twelve trains full of whistle,

past nihilist bamboo, growing regardless
of love's killing words and smiles, yet still
she can reach him here. Even never
looking back, he is already salt.

Imagining Charles Babbage and Ada Lovelace as Two Sides of a Quadratic Equation

Her eyes were black as a deepest forest night.
Her planed cheekbones hung taut as
rafters of a fine cathedral,
curved and yet angled to cut back the fog
around us. Her golden skin,
her deepening eyes
and the copper curls twirled
around her face like rain.
He can almost see the gold
of six wings crowning her head.
When erect they pull the air
and gravity away, help her bear with lightness
all his ideas. At night they fold in,
nestle close, portent of her intellect
as she dreams in French phrases
fanning dark insects away from her face.

Meanwhile, he is a head full of storm, leaf and feathers.
His engine is eating him and it will never finish.
He stares into the numbers the way she does, like a cat,
while ears perk up like a fox's, sure of the hunt ahead
and the hounds behind. He'll show them!
His head grows lithe, thin spidering branches
from the crown of his head and in fall they shed leaves
which he tucks behind his ears to keep a little longer.
Under a gold-green patina his eyes still laugh
behind the masking numbers of his face.

He could look at her all day of course.
He could think equations with her all night.

War is electric

I press my finger across the skid of swirl and oily glass.
All the dust of where I've been and bled, sheds and sticks:
hot pixels switching to pearls without notice. Oh, me.
I can smell bright colors and endearing rain.

Oh my. No matter what cells made the old phone sing;
what matters is how I touch it. Fingerprints must smear against smart.
What can a box of old light bulbs tell us? How to screw up
like fan blades in the dark. How to screw love in circles.

Yes, I still remember how your number rings.
Old habits die hard.

Debugger

She is the voice in his head
that follows his eyes
telling him what's not working:
"line 57, missing curved bracket",
"line 58, no semicolon."

The measure of a developer
is how he debugs his own brain
patiently, he thinks
as he curses and tweaks:
Set breakpoint. Hit run.

Still not working and now
the damn debugger
chooses now to say nothing.
Was it how he called the service,
did he use all the wrong arguments
its object doesn't take?
Women should come
with O'Reilly textbooks
he thinks, a Wikipedia entry,
something. Gotta keep looking
running and breaking
line by line carefully
or else it crashes down
and then she's gone.

Messaging the dead

I watch as the cursor glides across the screen
captured in a chat box, hesitating as in life,
or maybe it's just harder to get the Internet
where the dead are. They take turns typing
cryptic messages asking where I am, what
am I wearing, why did I talk more to *her*
instead of *him*. They use acronyms of texting
because each letter travels so far from
echoing minds to my nervous eyeballs.
They always pass the Turing test in triplicate.
When I ask how it is over there they evade
comparison: "unspeakable" "indescribable"
"neither hot nor cold, really." The dead
always miss me, but I am just another cursor
in the end, I could be anyone over here,
alive and well, trying to capture their footprints
as they try to capture mine. We cannot touch.
We think we understand. We type and type
worried to find that each has been talking
like the skim of a Ouija board's glide
only to our own twitches and fears
all this time.

Gin trickle

running
across the waving   light glints
       straining hard   very hard
capture a fly   in your hand
     let it go   unharmed

wash your face   and let a bee
        drop to settle on your forehead
pretending   it's not there   works for other [Xs]
   and won't sting you   eventually
concertina playing from the laptop   in the background
      how else do we escape?

each carnival of lights   wafts its popcorn at you.
you are looking for a soulmate   who will text you
      simultaneous
you are thinking   your computer is a girl
you only let   curious [Xs] touch it

bend in the wind   let them keep you employed and silent
buzz too loud like the bee   and they think you might sting.
play a dirty-faced game
      and you see why they ask for beautiful
strangers in their bar   snatching and grabbing what they can

Border lands

absorbed rain only to beat back hailstones
with a stick
fought the fountains' spray of sleep
           all water features are one water feature, in dreams

raincoats are a thing of the past, but they mark
      each deepening border of
skin scent and rubber-plastic

he took my hand inside both
   of his hands   *like a butterfly I fluttered madly*
vestigial tracings of math

Pythagorean theorems mark my belly
I'd pierce it for him   make triangles on skin

cross into the borderlands
knowing all needles
       thread to a hole

I hit the return key   *hard*
he hits the escape key   *harder*

180 #Accelerando

```
181   def set_thrust (self, on):
182       self.thrust = on
183       if on:
184       ship_thrust_sound.rewind ( )
185       ship_thrust_sound.play( )
186       else:
187       ship_thrust_sound.pause( )
```

Slouching like a velvet rope

Yesterday my name was power
adapter, toaster jockey, tag spinner.
Today it's anger and liquid mercury, evading reach.
Tomorrow I'll be breaking the rules by showing up,
elbows on the table, scared to my sneakers of getting fired —-
being the girl who leans forward into everyone's face
instead of ornamental. If you show me your newest
phone, I might brain you with mine;
dig out your skull and put a chip in, instead.
All a gadget wants is to be turned on and stroked,
lips against its glass surface, it reflects someone else's face.
A gadget is not a woman.
No one will notice that it isn't you in there.
Just like no one noticed that *my name isn't that girl*
And *I didn't come here from marketing,* I flew in
full frontal from engineering.

The mystery, explained

All day the lines fall across my face, strung
like piano wire through cortex. Each command
like whistling. My body floats above
my head, somewhere up and to the right.
I forget to pee and eat, curse hourly
how coffee gets cold. Each hard-won
hard-on inside the computer tested, tested,
then saved ultimately before the crash.

Finally, the lime-fresh smell of victory:
the rocket ship moves, the asteroids spin,
and lights like tiny stars explode across my face.

He is surprised how the bed rocks like a ship.
No gravity for this girl. He's surprised
to find me bouncing above him,
on his hips; grins to pull my lips down
as we grind through iterations, recursively.

"If I knew coding would make you this horny,"
he says, "I would have shown you Coursera
weeks ago."

All the walls of paper around us let us breathe

Bowed against the wooden frames bellied against the metal clasps and hinges we flutter like white moths, uncertain where our hands are, where that softness of skin backed by warm muscles will end.   Stretching now with the flutes of our finger bones and the soft drum pads of thumbs, we seek ways into crevices, sliding doors, whispers.   Under the bed, woven threads of tiny sheep hairs bring their heat.   Under the bed our cat rustles as he hears mountains shaking in the distance because erupting is too trite a word, laughter hanging light as lanterns around our bodies glowing outward in the dark.   Finally rhythmic, finally squared away. Always paper thin.

SECTION THREE

Avoid the dark corners of the language, including constructs that might be arguably legal but that are liable to confuse programmers, or even compilers.

#trying to draw explosions

```
def draw(self, canvas):
    if self.animated==True:
        canvas.draw_image(self.image,[self.image_center[0]+(64*self.
        age),self.image_center[1]], self.image_size,self.pos, self.image_
        size, self.angle)
    else:
        canvas.draw_image(self.image, self.image_center,self.image_size,
        self.pos, self.image_size, self.ang

def shoot(self):
    global Missile_group
        forward = angle_to_vector(self.angle)
        missile_pos = [self.pos[0] + self.radius * forward[0], self.pos[1] +
        self.radius * forward[1]]
        missile_vel = [self.vel[0] + 6 * forward[0], self.vel[1] + 6 *
        forward[1]]
        new_missile = Sprite(missile_pos, missile_vel, self.angle, 0,
        missile_image, missile_info, missile_sound)
        missile_group.add(new_missile)
```

Assembling language

You say, I'm getting out of this single-threaded apartment
while the getting is good. Your eyes
write the two of us,

memories in black boxes, stacked frames. Underneath,
your words writhe in hidden constructs,
operators:

Come with me. Stay here. Have sex, decide later.

I can choose what I set as pointer by memorizing
your black jeans, the way they crease
and fade in the sun

as you fidget, the way this conversation's sum
pushes values I'm not buying
into the bit bucket.

Programming languages
—for JHW

James says when he was nine
his father taught him the hard languages
spoken mostly by machines: metal cases open,
guts spilling to the pavement,
gloves handling parts on a greasy driveway.

Mistakes hardened his father's eyes,
green eyes that loved the circus stretch
of wires and the scruff of raised voices.
Mistakes toughened long hands that typed
the contoured textures of algorithms.

Coiled in sync, old bruises rising,
James tells me how he would wrestle
his father without speaking.
Focusing through a bottle, James will confess
the colors of numbers in his head,

how he codes the heart, never setting
shadows to zero, how one sharp axe
splits the sentence. Sparring for a frame
to put peace in, he grapples the ouroboros
twisting silicon through his childhood,

chases rubber snakes through boxes. James says
his computer screen is a mirror for sideshow.
The evil king muted, it fires line by line,
and makes itself up, bearded and smiling.
Twenty years later, James writes a letter to his father,

pushing for the verbs about the sudden blows,
stares at his mirrors, awaits word by dove
though his father is dead. James says
he can't say enough outside his father's earshot.
The dead have no fists. James says language

is like an investment banker in a biker bar
who's just grabbed a bottle by the bulge,
a semaphore of waving threats and cursing:
one hundred silent eyes in glass
waiting to see if he'll hit something.

Automata factory

1.
The only way you can get sick here
is if you bring it with you, messy fluids smeared
in fingerprints against the white diamond glass.
Breathe hoarse steam against vibrating steel grates.
Cough your flu unheard against the engines of the night.
The workers wear white masks and helmets
exoskeletons carve their sinews
into windup toys with silver capillaries.
Voices flit from radio to radio, barking orders
less human-looking than their handiwork.

This is the assembly line where they press down faces
for market; they start out cerise, taupe, green
and end up bronze, ebony, ivory, pink.
The faces they give you repel disease,
attract wealth, give off pheromones
that will linger in hallways. But you
will only speak the language of faces
once you put them on. The ears
are part of the deal and only buzz
in a certain range. The poor are gone

and you cannot smell them.
Only a humming like a refrigerator
constant and in the background
might make its way to your jaw.

Sometimes the face will clench and grind
your prosthetic teeth in the night.
You won't know it except in your bones.
No one would know anything
to look at you.

Breakpoint

A hawk drops like a stone to the rabbit, caught at a stop like the program.
Like the ship locks, letting water out to sea. Where we stop and all check
our backpacks, making sure we have enough water. It's a long climb up
before we can run.

All the signs were there

All the signs were there: sudden death
in the football matches, sudden death
on the highway with a lone gunman,
sudden death of anything she wanted
to stay at work for. Rounding the cabinets
of emergency medical supplies and Band-Aids
that were never up to the task of bleeding
from the brain out, she paces her own sweet time,
racing past the vending machines with
death on sugar sticks, cancer in bright packaging,
their promise of sweet, sweet forgetfulness for an hour
of dopamined-out bliss. How could she not know
before this that she raced for her life,
beating the elevator down the steps breathless
into the parking garage with its captured fumes
of a dragon, whose wise and wide yellow
fan eyes whirled slowly as they played the riddle game
of getting out of a space where the lines are drawn,
of getting out while the going is still good and elastic,
of getting through the door before night falls on skids
escaping before the body freezes into plastic.

Persephone's tech nightmare

When she awakens she knows she hasn't really escaped,
she's still wandering in the nightmare of machines
and blood-silence. Radio waves wave their tiny fingers
through her bones and she feels the frequency shift
ever higher out of earshot. The lights know to turn on
when she walks into the room because they are
not real servants, not real men, not real big
when it comes right down to it. Their smarts
are smaller than a baby's fist, she could put them
in her pocket and be able to light up the room.

In the nightmare of machines it is always light
because the baby's fist and cry can make it so;
the little radio on her nightstand talks to a baby
that isn't there, an empty crib. (Another part
of the nightmare is the story that isn't hers,
regrets she's never had, weaving into this
waterfall of dreaming loss). When she awakens
she will be sure she mislaid a child somewhere
but for now she is following the web strand
of machines through this sleepwalk
that is not her apartment

not her old family house with its creaking shutters
and railroad trains that went by on the hour.
She is following the long hallway to the heartbeat
of this dream which somehow leads to her death
and a coffin like a tanning booth rises up from the shag rug;

a set of steps inside, a metal mall escalator
whose grooved steps bite in their gears only hot metal
and it jerks taut, and she is falling down into the dark
of the stairwell. Clenched and released she awakens
startled on her bed, hours before the alarm machines
wanted her waking. Clutching the sheets
sure she has been sent a sign of destiny or duty.
But what child, what coffin, what heinous fall?

Stolen around her shoulders

In her dream she met him in his apartment that had been an old mechanics'
    garage.
The bed was still on a lift that could be pulled up and down but they
sat on the couch while the bed floated above some far corner.
Huge windows stared in at them like eyes. She had come seeking
his advice or some reassurance she was in the right neighborhood
for this dream. And he simply had dragged her into this apartment,
sure in what he had to say: *she should be here.*
They snuggled on the couch, with him
breathing so gently into the back of her neck, waiting in the silence
for her to calm and for the square walls of this place to lift.
It wasn't about bed, his body told her, though there was that too.
It wasn't about being light outside, or inside for that matter,
she still fluttered like a mad bird, hummingbird mind going and going.
It was about the kiss on the neck that said, *take your time baby*
while the dark walls were still around them and she didn't know the door.

Autosuggest

Give me two letters, maybe three, and I can make
I am into *I am awaiting, I am trying to lose weight,*
I am weightless. Or more commonly speaking
I am a gummy bear, I am *a man of constant sorrow,*
a man of god, a man more sinned against than sinning.

Give me a word or three and I can tell
probabilities of what people want to hear
within a couple thousand finger taps, *don't leave me,*
don't leave me hanging on, don't leave me hanging
on by my fingernails. Hot coals I lean over every day
just trying to get the words out without getting burned,
who wouldn't grab the lifejacket of the back button
word bucket, search box, cell phone,
type and try again, stammering suggestively.

Give me a motif and a melody now and I'd sing that song
you wanted to hear, charge you ninety-nine cents
for nights of listening, over and over. Words like
There's an empty space in the garage and over the roof,
words like *cramped into one corner of the bed*
even as the sheets open wide. Empty breathing
is my own breath, and the stammer-struck beat
alone is the suggestion that something
must change, something must spill out past.
There must be some new result for this.

[X_] plays Planescape Torment

I am not a girl.
I am always waking up somewhere
completely gross. In this case an undead
factory complete with me, product #257
(or whatever the tag said, I lost it). The smell
of the talking skull isn't so bad, just the rest
of me feels rubbery and old.
When they say the tang of copper blood
they mean this place, which is a mine of pain,
a staircase of creaking bones, an ever-present
stone furnace that could end my misery presumably.
But it just doesn't get that easy.

The hero eternal has a bad haircut.
The hero eternal is sort of a lunkhead, but
he's me, and I try to play him faithful to the part
complete with reading all my former skins
stretched like drumheads on the wall.
Or maybe I'm just the eternal bro
doomed to wander the world looking
for high fives and bandages, a new girlfriend
and more bandages and unable to defeat myself
properly, or look myself in the eye.

The Sketcher, the Witcher

1. She has a silver sword she's not afraid to use. And a black crow feather tucked behind her white, white hair. And a potion flask of the blackest ink. Some say it was sorcery, that turned a young woman's hair white before her time. When asked what she does, in every bar from here to elvish country, she says: I kill monsters.

2. Men step back when she looks up at them, bent over the corpse of the town's favorite whore. The two puncture wounds on the throat, the obvious trust in letting the murderer in – no forced doors. And the blood, blood everywhere on the sheets. The Sketcher draws out the crime scene on the parchment, the positions of the onlookers, all the shredded tatters of silk. The men have brought garlic, ropes of papery globes they wear around their necks. The Sketcher laughs.

3. Every time she beds a man in town, she draws his picture, while he's sleeping. Nude, so many look alike but she tries to add some flair to remember them by – gold chains float around the banker, beakers between the legs of the alchemist, arrows notching the bed of the guard tower archer. When she leaves, she pastes them to the inside of a place other women will see – the kitchen of the castle, the closets of a bordello, an outhouse farthest from town that the women all use. Penis sizes are not augmented.

4. If it's a new town, she usually has to prove her blade works; if there are too many attackers she casts black pepper in their eyes. So many years in the kitchen, she could press raw onions and pepper to her eyes with one hand and keep slicing. So many years on the road, a lone crow cawing.

5. She catches a man following one of the women on her way to the outhouse. Like all of the townsmen he wears an ineffective necklace of garlic. But he's also got a nasty two-pronged iron pitchfork. The outhouse door is open, the woman with her skirts up, screaming.

6. She leaps forward as the woman screams from the outhouse's open door, knocking him off balance, two prongs splintering the wood. A silvered stab to the kidneys. Black flies are buzzing around the Sketcher's sweaty forehead. She wants to forget this picture, but she will be drawing it over and over in her sleep.

7. The young woman asks her to stay and live happily ever after. Wolves and bears prowl their farm, and she could use a strong hand about the place. The Sketcher sighs, hands her the un-used two-pronged pitchfork. I only kill monsters, the Sketcher says.

8. The next day she is gone, but she leaves on the woman's door a rather fine charcoal nude sketch of the town's grateful mayor.

Fabulous numbers

They are fake, these rocks and   perfection
in craggy purposefulness,   caged in pristine
glass that never breaks or soots.   Propane feeds the flames
which are real and burn clean.   Around the square of light
is the other square of night;   our talk folded and unfolded
like long legs and napkins.   Outside even that set of edges
coyotes
and even a bobcat may prowl.   Outside even bobcats
run the wild rings of the stars.   And the fake
rocks powered by our concerns   flame on.
It is not necessary to be real.

The women's room at [variable1] tech conference in [variable2] city

The toilet seats are U-shaped sentinels
of the sparkling clean you can expect.
For some reason they are all up,

like expecting an army of men
to come pee there; but there's only you.
As you walk you have your choice

of any stall, pick a stall, to lower
and hover over, not sure what
kind of bleach will be staining

your thighs. You can bleed
and hold your gut as long as you want.
Wrap it all in a sanitary bag,

crinkle as loudly as you like.
Outside, men will scratch their balls
through their jeans, forgetting

you are there. Outside, you
are the outsider crashing and crinkling
the world of men. But in this moment,

four walls stand firm for women like you
and you are here for a mirror
to give your game face a break.

Blazon for a computer

1.

my computer with its cords of the medusa, with its snake-wriggling nodes
    around the carpet, plugs hot to the touch with its shadows of soft dark
    napkins half in glare, half in twilight

my computer with its long-boned monitor, base of black and silver
    capturing
stability in a horseshoe with its long tongues of adapters lapping electric
into my spilled coffee with their tiny tiny teeth

with its giant square eye that blinks   so fast you can't tell if it's crying
 of no words following   the dare of the backlit keys

my computer with its nervous fingers in my mind, whispers
in my head, promises of what can carry me
into bullet trains, into clouds

of perfumed music, screen of tiny stars   brightest thing in a room
    full of doubts

2.
if I gave up my computer I would be giving up all the copies of myself
I left thinking they would be enough.

Search engine

There is Cassandra twanging like a string
inside a room bought and paid for by someone else.
She is hungry and she is everywhere
the Internet does not go. When she is beaten
in the night there are no selfies, no marches,
no twitter hashtags to make it right.

When the police arrive at another domestic
she might be recorded, but nothing pops up next to his name,
the one who brought her here from her mother's house.
The Web is silent. She is unindexed and the people
at the café look away from her face.

What the search engine will not find
is the next part:
bleeding, running, the escape
to another state where he would not know to follow.
When she founds a startup to help battered women
she trains with a gun; she is ready for men like him
to be found.

Everything around us opens with time

1.

Yes, everything around us opens
with time. Feel it in the tug
at the end of the runway. Always
one last part of a plane about to leave
the ground feels the catch –
the final drag and exhale.
Then plastic cups wet gin
into the sky and out the portals
we see the curve over the wind-carved ocean.
Below us, unseen, the city sparks the city.

2.

These buildings are all square-cornered lies.
Like yeses, all the windows blink as a mood streams
out of that air box into newly cupped hands,
central parks, open carts. I've met more people
in orange sunglasses that all turned out
to be me, lost, with maps in their hands.
Smiling and waving we become each train
of thought leaving empty track in its wake.
Steel and rubber intentions always leave the platform
under swaying feet, while out windows hands palm the welcoming
only to release it in goodbye after goodbye. Over and over
the metal wheels sing their songs of open skies
and subjugated prairie (because everything around us
opens, in time) and so golden, we whistle our lives
defiantly into the rushing dark.

#Function of the self

```
def update(self):
        # update angle
        self.angle += self.angle_vel

        # update position
        self.pos[0] = (self.pos[0] + self.vel[0]) % WIDTH
        self.pos[1] = (self.pos[1] + self.vel[1]) % HEIGHT

        #update age
        self.age = self.age+1
        if self.age < self.lifespan:
            return False
        else:
                        return True
```

Notes

Sections breaks are quoted from Herb Sutter's *Exceptional C++ Style: 40 New Engineering Puzzles, Programming Problems and Solutions* and Christopher Moore and Stephan Merten's *The Nature of Computation*.

"The tires hold the road on their rims" is after *"All Pumped Up"* a painting by Manon Sander shown at the Cornell Museum, Delray Beach, Florida.

"Subverting the language," "The decimal is a heartbeat; it can stop itself or repeat" were both inspired by Sutter's *Exceptional C++ Style: 40 New Engineering Puzzles, Programming Problems, and Solutions.*

"Do I look like I code?" was inspired by "Silent Technical Privilege," by Philip Guo, *The Atlantic* Jan. 15, 2014.

The found "code poems" are excerpted from Python game code I wrote for *An Introduction to Interactive Programming in Python*, created by Rice University for Coursera.com. (I highly recommend this course as hard but fun!) Other poems about the art of programming were code reviewed as necessary.

Poems about yōkai and other Japanese spirits were inspired by entries in *The Hour of Meeting Evil Spirits: an Encyclopedia of Mononoke and Magic* by Matthew Meyer.

Acknowledgments

An earlier version of "The Tires Hold the Road On Their Rims" was published online as an Honorable Mention at the Palm Beach Poetry Festival's Plein Air Contest in 2015.

"Walking here is to be swallowed by the sky" first appeared in in the *Southern Humanities Review* issue 51.3 as a finalist for the 2017 Auburn Witness Poetry Prize.

"Okuri Inu or the sending-off dog demon" was originally published in *Uncanny Magazine* Issue #22, May/June 2018 and reprinted in the 2019 Rhysling Anthology as part of being nominated for a Rhysling award that year.

"The decimal is a heartbeat; it can stop itself or repeat," formerly known as "Destruction," and "Encapsulation in computer programming" appeared in both print and online versions of the *Carbon Culture Review* in 2015.

"Buruburu" was originally published in *Uncanny Magazine*, Issue #29, July/August 2019.

"What to expect from the Hadron Collider as a college roommate" was originally published in *Uncanny Magazine*, Issue #16, May/June 2017.

"A tenjō kudari ("ceiling hanger" yōkai) defends her theft" originally published in *Uncanny Magazine* Issue #32, January/February 2020.

"For a heartbeat" (2009) and "All the signs were there" (2013) appeared in *The Comstock Review* as finalists for the Muriel Craft Bailey Award.

"War is electric" first appeared as "Old Habits Die Hard" in *Enizagam* Vol. 9, 2015.

"Messaging the Dead" is scheduled to appear in *Asimov's Science Fiction Magazine* for its January/February 2022 issue.

"Slouching like a velvet rope" was first published in issue 54.3 of *Southern Humanities Review* and selected by Jericho Brown as the winner of the 2021 Auburn Witness Poetry Prize.

An earlier version of "All the walls of paper around us let us breathe," appeared as "Shōji Screens" in the *Nimrod International Journal of Prose and Poetry,* Spring/Summer 2017.

"Automata Factory" appeared in *The Nassau Review* and selected for a 2015 Writer Award.

An earlier version of "Stolen around her shoulders" appeared in the online *Pontoon Poetry* Issue #11 as "Thursday Night Dream."

"Everything around us opens with time" first appeared in the anthology *Fire On Her Tongue: an eBook Anthology of Contemporary Women's Poetry,* (edited by Kelli Russell Agodon and Annette Spaulding-Convy), Two Sylvias Press, 2012.

Special Thanks

To Dorothy Barresi who gave *Breakpoint* its cybernetic wings and Alexandra Umlas who guided it through liftoff. Thank you Tebot Bach!

To Jericho Brown, grateful thanks for elevating the voice of a coder girl.

To my parents, Drs. Susan and Thomas Aoki.

To Jason McCullough, for all the code reviews, love and lattes.

For the evolution of the manuscript, much appreciation to:
Kimiko Hahn, who saw the Xbox poem and told me to write more
Colleen J. McElroy, who advised: "Coder girl takes over."

Other literary instigators:
Neil Aitken, Allen Braden, Kelly Clayton, Ashley C. Ford, Lorraine Healy, Alan Chong Lau, Denise Miller, Kristin Naca, Sally J. Pla, Derek Sheffield, Jan Wallace and The Clarion West Class of 2016 (Team Arsenic!)

Non-profit organizations:
Many of these poems would not have been written without the space and time afforded by Hedgebrook's Writer in Residence, and the six-week residency at Clarion West Writers Workshop. Grateful thanks are also due to Artist Trust and the City of Seattle for generous grants that enabled further writing time.

About the Author

Elizabeth (Betsy) Aoki is a poet, fiction writer and video game producer. Her first poetry collection, *Breakpoint* was a 2019 National Poetry Series Finalist and published by Tebot Bach as the winner of the Patricia Bibby First Book Award. Its signature poem "Slouching like a velvet rope" won the 2021 Auburn Witness Poetry Prize, selected by Jericho Brown.

Aoki has received grants and fellowships from the City of Seattle, Artist Trust Foundation, Jackstraw Writers Program, Clarion West Writers Workshop and Hedgebrook. Her chapbook, *Every Vanish Leaves Its Trace*, was published by Finishing Line Press. Other publications include *Calyx, Hunger Mountain, Nassau Review* (winner of the 2015 Writer Award), the *Nimrod International Journal of Prose and Poetry, Phoebe, Poetry Northwest, The Seattle Times, Seattle Review, Southern Humanities Review, terrain.org (Letters to America)*, and *Uncanny Magazine*.

You can find her tweeting at @baoki or contact her via her website at betsyaoki.com.

TEBOT BACH
A 501 (c) (3) Literary Arts Education Non Profit

THE TEBOT BACH MISSION: advancing literacy, strengthening
community, and transforming life experiences with the power of poetry
through readings, workshops, and publications.

THE TEBOT BACH PROGRAMS
1. A poetry reading and writing workshop series for venues such as homeless
shelters, battered women's shelters, nursing homes, senior citizen daycare
centers, Veterans organizations, hospitals, AIDS hospices, correctional
facilities which serve under-represented populations. Participating poets
include: John Balaban, Brendan Constantine, Megan Doherty, Richard Jones,
Dorianne Laux, M.L. Leibler, Laurence Lieberman, Carol Moldaw, Patricia
Smith, Arthur Sze, Carine Topal, Cecilia Woloch.

2. A poetry reading and writing workshop series for the community Southern
California at large, and for schools K-University. The workshops feature
local, national, and international teaching poets; David St. John, Charles
Webb, Wanda Coleman, Amy Gerstler, Patricia Smith, Holly Prado, Dorothy
Lux, Rebecca Seiferle, Suzanne Lummis, Michael Datcher, B.H. Fairchild,
Cecilia Woloch, Chris Abani, Laurel Ann Bogen, Sam Hamill, David Lehman,
Christopher Buckley, Mark Doty.

3. A publishing component to give local, national, and international poets a
venue for publishing and distribution.

Tebot Bach
Box 7887
Huntington Beach, CA 92615-7887
714-968-0905
www.tebotbach.org